Silver Threads

Donna McCarthy

W9-BEX-478

Maxfield Parrish

A
PRICE GUIDE

Stephanie Lane

Copyright 1993

L-W Book Sales
Box 69
Gas City, IN 46933

ISBN: 0-89538-014-5

Table of Contents

ACKNOWLEDGEMENTS

I would like to thank the following for the help they have given on this book.

Jon Alk, 2606 River Lane, Green Bay, Wisconsin 54301. Jon furnished many pictures and so much of his knowledge. We are deeply indebted for <u>ALL</u> his help.

Gwen Goldman, 4 Michael Lane, Denver, Pennsylvania 17517. Gwen has helped us on many books dealing with paper. She is probably the most knowledgable dealer in the U.S. on paper, prints, and ephemera. Gwen, all of us in the editoral department want to thank you very much.

Thanks to collector Michael Goldberg, Rochester, New York and his photographer Len Rosenberg, 2077 Clinton Avenue, Rochester, New York.

Portal Press, Corte Madera, California for pictures from their archives. Thanks.

Maxfield Parrish
BACKGROUND
By Pat Campbell

To some, Maxfield Parrish was an artist. To others, he was a magician, extracting dreams from some untouched childhood memory and setting it free upon any surface he might have been working on at the time. With his use of vibrant colors set within a subtle framework of aged architecture and brilliant landscapes, his sense of capturing the imagination onto each piece brought about his reputation as that of a master. Flawless yet distinctly human, his legacy of prints and paintings still today recapture those feelings of awe. A craftsman who opened windows to the world of dreams and disguised them as paintings, Maxfield Parrish remains a generous man, leaving us with many wonderful images in his absence.

The legacy itself began on July 25, 1870 in Philadelphia. Stephen and Elizabeth Parrish brought home a new son, Frederick Parrish. Later adopting his mother's maiden name, Maxfield, as his middle name, this was the title that would accompany each piece, and the title Maxfield Parrish is the one recognized as this magnificent artist. Parrish was very fortunate as a youth to have traveled Europe with his parents on various trips. This brought about his early appreciation of the Arts, particularly Painting, Architecture, and Music. Nudged further by his father, whose interest in Art led to a career of printing and etching, Maxfield's style and artistic identity soon began to form.

Maxfield's schooling included Haverford College & the Pennsylvania Academy of Fine Arts, plus a brief tenure as a pupil of Howard Pyle at the Drexel Institute. He spent his early summers sharing a seaside studio with his father in Annisquam, Massachusetts. The Philadelphia Art Club was the first to host a Maxfield Parrish oil painting exhibit in 1893, with the piece **Moonrise** portrayed in this exhibit. Harper's Bazaar magazine was the first publication to introduce Maxfield as a coverpiece designer in 1895. This led to many assignments for magazine coverpieces, with his resume later including works published by Collier's, Scribner's, Century Magazine, Life and Ladies Home Journal. Maxfield Parrish's series of cover designs for these and other publications gained him his nationwide recognition as a truly inspired American artist. In 1897, Maxfield was elected to be a member of the Society of American Artists, alongside his exhibit of **The Sandman.**

Despite recurring bouts with tuberculosis, Maxfield Parrish introduced many pieces throughout the early 1900's which found themselves cast as advertisements, calendar artwork, book illustrations, murals, and much more. He remained at his studio "The Oaks", in

Cornish, New Hampshire, for many years while he continued his painting career. His studio time during these years were often interrupted with Maxfield's many travels throughout the United States and much of Europe, gaining inspiration and insight which found life through the paintings he created during these years. Further inspiration during his lifetime was his family, three sons, a daughter, and his wife Lydia. Not only recognized as a painter, his interest in architecture and his representation of the fantastic structures in his images led him to his Medal of Honor awarded to him by the Architectural League of New York in 1917. Parrish was decorated by others as well during his life as a renowned illustrator. An elected member in the National Academy of Design and the Philadelphia Water Color Club, he also accepted an honorary LL.D. from his former school, Haverford College, in 1914. The University of New Hampshire decorated Parrish as an honorary Doctor of Fine Arts in 1954. Exhibitions across the country allowed many people to witness his artwork firsthand throughout his painting years.

On March 30, 1966, the last chapter of Maxfield Parrish's illustrious legend commenced. His death at age ninety-five at his studio in Cornish was an end to the production of his paintings. Yet, his legend still thrives to this day, as countless Maxfield Parrish admirers still relish the prints, posters, and pictures which bear his infinite imagination. The unending search to discover prints and collectibles which sustain his illustrations has included many participants eager to witness a new addition to their Maxfield Parrish collection. This book was published with these people in mind, to ensure that they have a source to help continue their search.

Magazine Covers

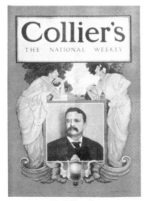

Collier's
March 4, 1905

Collier's
July 22, 1905

Collier's
September 23, 1905

Collier's
October 14, 1905

Magazine Covers

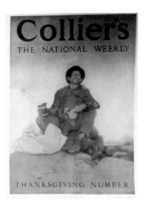

Collier's
November 18, 1905

Collier's
December 16, 1905

Collier's
May 19, 1906

Collier's
November 17, 1906

Magazine Covers

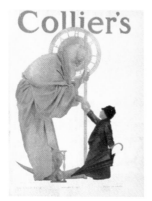

**Collier's
January 5, 1907**

**Collier's
May 11, 1929**

**Collier's
October 24, 1936**

**Collier's
December 26, 1936**

Magazine Covers

Scribner's – December 1901

Scribner's – October 1900

Scribner's – December 1900

Magazine Covers

Ladies Home Journal – May 1913

**Ladies Home Journal
June 1930**

**Ladies Home Journal
April 1921**

Magazine Covers

Collier's
January 6, 1906

Collier's
March 10, 1906

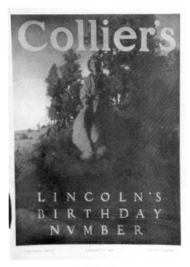

Collier's
February 10, 1906

Magazine Covers

Collier's
July 21, 1906

Collier's
June 23, 1906

Collier's
July 7, 1906

Magazine Covers

**Collier's
April 15, 1905**

**Collier's
May 6, 1905**

Magazine Covers

Scribner's – April 1899

Scribner's – August 1899

Magazine Covers

Collier's
July 1, 1905

Collier's
October 28, 1905

Magazine Covers

Ladies Home Journal
January 1931

Collier's
April 24, 1909

Magazine Covers

Scribner's – December 1895

Ladies Home Journal – July 1912

Magazine Covers

**Scribner's
December 1897**

Ladies Home Journal – July 1906

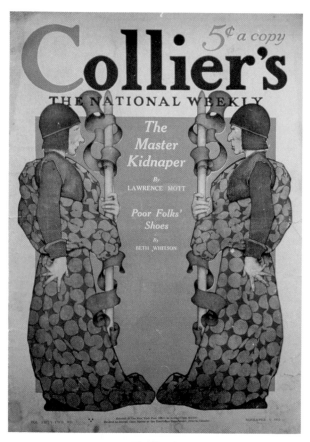

Collier's
November 1, 1913

Magazine Covers

Ladies Home Journal
September 1904

**Ladies Home Journal
June 1901**

Magazine Covers

**The Outing
September 1905**

Magazine Covers

**Scribner's
October 1904**

Success
December 1901

Magazine Covers

1. Agricultural Digest – November, 1934
2. Book Buyer – December, 1897
3. Book Buyer – December, 1898
4. Book Buyer – April, 1899
5. Book Buyer – December, 1899
6. Booknews – October, 1895
7. Booknews – November, 1895
8. Booknews – December, 1895
9. Booknews – January, 1896
10. Booknews – March, 1896
11. Booknews – March, 1897
12. Booknews – April, 1897
13. Booknews – June, 1897
14. Century – December, 1914
15. Century – August, 1917
16. Collier's – December 3, 1904
17. Collier's – January 7, 1905
18. Collier's – February 11, 1905
19. Collier's – March 4, 1905
20. Collier's – April 15, 1905
21. Collier's – May 6, 1905
22. Collier's – May 20, 1905
23. Collier's – June 3, 1905
24. Collier's – July 1, 1905
25. Collier's – July 8, 1905
26. Collier's – July 22, 1905
27. Collier's – August 5, 1905
28. Collier's – September 23, 1905
29. Collier's – October 14, 1905
30. Collier's – October 28, 1905
31. Collier's – November 4, 1905
32. Collier's – November 18, 1905
33. Collier's – December 2, 1905
34. Collier's – December 16, 1905
35. Collier's – January 6, 1906
36. Collier's – February 10, 1906
37. Collier's – March 3, 1906
38. Collier's – March 10, 1906
39. Collier's – May 19, 1906
40. Collier's – June 23, 1906
41. Collier's – July 7, 1906
42. Collier's – July 21, 1906
43. Collier's – November 17, 1906
44. Collier's – January 5, 1907
45. Collier's – March, 1907
46. Collier's – November 30, 1907
47. Collier's – June 6, 1908
48. Collier's – July 4, 1908

Magazine Covers

49. Collier's – July 18, 1908
50. Collier's – August 8, 1908
51. Collier's – September 12, 1908
52. Collier's – December 12, 1908
53. Collier's – December 26, 1908
54. Collier's – January 2, 1909
55. Collier's – March 20, 1909
56. Collier's – April 3, 1909
57. Collier's – April 17, 1909
58. Collier's – April 24, 1909
59. Collier's – May 1, 1909
60. Collier's – May 29, 1909
61. Collier's – June 26, 1909
62. Collier's – July 3, 1909
63. Collier's – July 10, 1909
64. Collier's – July 24, 1909
65. Collier's – November 20, 1909
66. Collier's – December 11, 1909
67. Collier's – January 8, 1910
68. Collier's – July 30, 1910
69. Collier's – September 3, 1910
70. Collier's – September 24, 1910
71. Collier's – November 26, 1910
72. Collier's – February 4, 1911
73. Collier's – April 1, 1911
74. Collier's – March 11, 1911
75. Collier's – March 18, 1911
76. Collier's – September 30, 1911
77. Collier's – November 2, 1912
78. Collier's – November 16, 1912
79. Collier's – May 10, 1913
80. Collier's – May 17, 1913
81. Collier's – November 1, 1913
82. Collier's – January 5, 1929
83. Collier's – May 11, 1929
84. Collier's – July 20, 1929
85. Collier's – November 30, 1929
86. Collier's – October 24, 1936
87. Collier's – December 26, 1936
88. Country Life – March, 1908
89. Current Literature – 1893
90. Harper's Bazaar – December, 1895
91. Harper's Bazaar – March, 1914
92. Harper's Monthly – December, 1896
93. Harper's Monthly – December 1900
94. Harper's Round Table – July, 1895
95. Harper's Round Table – August, 1895
96. Harper's Round Table – November, 1895

Magazine Covers

Magazine Covers

144. Life – August 25, 1921
145. Life – October 13, 1921
146. Life – November 10, 1921
147. Life – December 1, 1921
148. Life – January 5, 1922
149. Life – April 6, 1922
150. Life – May 11, 1922
151. Life – June 22, 1922
152. Life – July 20, 1922
153. Life – August 24, 1922
154. Life – October 19, 1922
155. Life – December 7, 1922
156. Life – March 1, 1923
157. Life – March 29, 1923
158. Life – August 30, 1923
159. Life – January 31, 1924
160. Magazine Of Light – February, 1931
161. Magazine Of Light – Summer, 1931
162. Magazine Of Light – Summer, 1932
163. McClure's Monthly – November, 1904
164. McClure's Monthly – January, 1905
165. McClure's Monthly – February, 1905
166. McClure's Monthly – March, 1905
167. McClure's Monthly – May, 1905
168. McClure's Monthly – July, 1906
169. McClure's Monthly – October, 1906
170. McClure's Monthly – January, 1907
171. Metropolitan – January, 1917
172. Minnesota Journal of Education –
     July, 1925
173. Nebraska Educational Journal –
     October, 1928
174. New England Homestead –
     January 2, 1897
175. New Hampshire Troubadour –
     1938: Yearbook
176. New Hampshire Troubadour –
     1939: Fair Edition
177. New Hampshire Troubadour –
     February, 1940
178. Osteopathic Magazine – July, 1925
179. Outing – June, 1900
180. Outing – July, 1900
181. Outing – August, 1900
182. Outing – September, 1900
183. Outing – October, 1900
184. Outing – November, 1900
185. Outing – December, 1900

Magazine Covers

186. Outing – January, 1901
187. Outing – February, 1901
188. Outing – May, 1901
189. Outing – November, 1904
190. Outing – January, 1905
191. Outing – February, 1905
192. Outing – April, 1905
193. Outing – May, 1905
193a. Outing – September, 1905
194. Outing – September, 1906
195. Outing - November, 1906
196. Outing – December, 1906
197. Outing – May, 1907
198. Outing – July, 1907
199. Outing – October, 1907
200. Outing – November, 1907
201. Outing – June, 1908
202. Outing – September, 1908
203. Outing – October, 1908
204. Outing – November, 1908
205. Outing – April, 1909
206. Outing – February, 1909
207. Outing – March, 1909
208. Outing – July, 1912
209. Progressive Farmer – June, 1952
209a. Scribner's – December, 1895
210. Scribner's – December, 1897
211. Scribner's – April, 1898
212. Scribner's – August, 1899
213. Scribner's – October, 1899
214. Scribner's – December, 1899
215. Scribner's – October, 1900
216. Scribner's – December, 1900
217. Scribner's – August, 1901
218. Scribner's – December, 1901
219. Scribner's – October, 1904
220. Scribner's – August, 1923
221. Scribner's New Books For
     The Young – 1898
222. Scribner's New Books for
     The Young – 1900
223. Success – December, 1901
224. Yankee – December, 1935
225. Yankee – December, 1968
226. Youths Companion– February 20, 1919
227. Youths Companion – January 3, 1924

Books

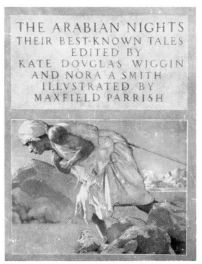

The Arabian Nights
1909

Poems of Childhood
1904

The Golden Treasury of
Songs and Lyrics
1911

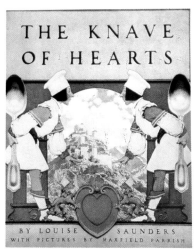

The Knave of Hearts
1925

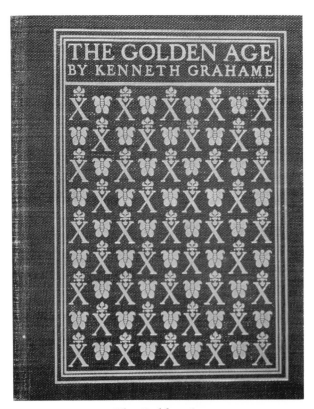

The Golden Age
1900

Books

228. A Loiterer in New York, Doran – 1917
229. A Saga Of The Seas – 1901
230. A Tuscan Childhood – Cipriana, 1907
231. Achievement In Photo Engraving – 1927
232. American Art By American Artists – 1898
233. American Arts – Rand McNally & Co., 1928
234. American Pictures & Painters – John Lane, 1917
235. American Poster, The – 1967
236. American Spirit In Art, The – Mather, 1927
237. Annual Of Advertising Art, The – 1921
238. Arabian Nights – Wiggins & Smith, 1909
239. Art & The Great War – Gallatin, 1919
240. Artist Yearbook, The – Hosking, 1905
241. Bolanyo – Read, 1897
242. Children's Books – Scudder, 1901
243. Collect. Of Color Prints, A – Guerin &
       Parish, 1920's
244. Collection of Parrish Illustrated Work &
       Related Ephemera – De Victor
245. Contemp. Illust. Of Childrens Books –
       Mahony, 1930
246. Dream Days – Lane, 1898
247. Early Years of Maxfield Parrish Sketches
248. Emerald Storybook, The – Skinner, 1915
249. Free To Serve – Copeland & Day, 1899
250. Garden Years & Poems – G.P. Putmans, 1904
251. Golden Age, The – Lane, 1900
252. Golden Treasury of Songs & Lyrics –
       Palgrave, 1911
253. Graphic Arts & Crafts Yearbook – Meadon, 1907
254. Great Magazine Covers Of The World –
       Kery, 1982
255. History Of Ideals & Art – Neuhaus, 1931
256. Home University Bookshelf – 1927-1948
257. Illustrated Book, The – Weitenampf, 1938
258. Illustrator In America, The – Reed, 1966
259. Illustrators Of Children's Books –
       Horn Books, 1947
260. International Library Of Music – Louis, 1925
261. Italian Villas & Their Gardens – Wharton, 1904
262. Jello Cookbooks – 1924
263. King Alberts Book – Caine, 1914
264. Knave Of Hearts (spiral bound) – 1925
265. Knave Of Hearts, The – Sanders, 1925
266. Knave Of Hearts Engagement Book – 1989
267. Knickerbockers History Of NY – Irving, 1900

Books

268. L. A. Architectural: Yearbook – 1911
269. Letters & Lettering – Brown, 1912
270. Loiterer In New York, A – Henderson, 1917
271. Lure Of The Garden – Putmans, 1911
272. Maxfield Parrish – Ludwig, 1973
273. Maxfield Parrish – The Early Years – Skeeters, 1973
274. Maxfield Parrish, Prints by Sweeney – 1974
275. Mother Goose In Prose – Baum, 1897
276. Palgraves, Golden Treasury of Song – 1911
277. P's & Q's – Tannahill, 1927
278. Pearl Storybook, The – Skinner, 1919
279. Peterkin – Jackson, 1912
280. Pictures By Popular American Artists – N.Y., 1900
281. Poems Of Childhood – Scribner's, 1904
282. Posters & Their Designers – Jones, 1924
283. Posters In Miniature – Russell, 1897
284. Posters, A Critical Study – Price, 1913
285. Price Guide to Maxfield Parrish – Jackson yearly
286. Printing Art, The – U. of Mass., 1910-1911
287. Romantic America – Schauffler, 1913
288. Ruby Storybook, The – Skinner, 1916
289. Sapphire Storybook, The – Skinner, Teens
290. Song of Haiwatha – Longfellow, 1912
291. Stories Of Chivalry – 1913
292. Survey – 1929
293. Thirty Favorite Paintings – 1908
294. This Fabulous Century – Time Life Books, 1969
295. Topaz Story, The – Skinner
296. Troubadour Tales – Stein, 1903
297. Turquoise Cup & The Desert – Smith 1903
298. Turquoise Storybook, The – Skinner, 1918
299. Watercolour Renderings – Parrish & Guerin, 1920's
300. Whist Reference Book – 1912
301. Wonderbook Of Tanglewood Tales – Hawthorne, 1910
302. You and Your Work – 1944

Posters

303. Adlake Camera: 1897
304. Century: 1897
305. Century: 1902
306. Columbia Bicycle: 1896 – Male Rider
307. Columbia Bicycle: 1896 – Female Rider
308. Edison-Mazda: Mid 1920's – 3ft. Knave, stand up poster
309. Edison – Mazda: Mid 1920's – EM Knave, Posters; 12" x 18"
310. Ferry Seeds: 19" x 19" – Peter Pumpkin Eater – 1918
311. Ferry Seeds: 19" x 19" – Peter Piper – 1919
312. Ferry Seeds: 19" x 19" – Mary, Mary – 1921
313. Ferry Seeds: 19" x 19" – Jack & The Beanstalk – 1923
314. Ferry Seeds: 19" x 19" – Man Standing by Fireplace
315. Fisk Tires: Window Cards – Magic Shoes – 1917
316. Fisk Tires: Window Cards – Fit For a King – 1917
317. Fisk Tires: Window Cards – Mother Goose – 1919
318. Fisk Tires: Window Cards - The Magic Circle – 1919
319. Hires Root Beer – 1920: small stand up
320. Hires Root Beer – 1920: large stand up
321. Heliotype Printing: 1896 – Child Harvester – 28" x 42"
322. Hornsby Oatmeal - 1896 Poster – 28" x 42"
323. Jell-O – 1920's - King & Queen Stand Up 29" x 34"
324. National Academy of Design: 1899 – 14 1/2" x 22" Tri-tones
325. National Authority on Amateur Sport – 1897 Harpers, 14 1/2" x 8 1/2"
326. New Hampshire State Planning – 1936 Thy Templed Hills – 24" x 29"
327. New Hampshire State Planning – 1939 N.H. Winter Paradise 24" x 29"
328. No-To-Bac: 1896
329. Philadelphia Horse Show: 1896
330. Swifts Ham: Mid 1920's – Jack Spratt

Prints

White Birch – 1931

Spring – 1911

Harvest – 1905

Stars – 1926

Prints

Canyon
March 29, 1924

Wynken, Blynken, & Nod
1905

Wild Geese – 1924

Hilltop – 1927

Prints

Cleopatra – 1917

King of The Black Isles 1907

The Prince – 1928

Prints

Dreaming – 1928

The Lute Players – 1924

Garden of Allah – 1918

Prints

Midsummer Holiday Number
August 1897

Poster Show – 1896

Easter – 1905

Prints

**The Golden Treasury of
Songs and Lyrics
1911**

Twilight – 1901

Prints

Daybreak – 1922

Prints

The Dinkey Bird – 1905

Prints

The Lantern Bearers – December 10, 1910

Prints

Reinthal & Newman

331. Broadmoor Hotel, The – 1915: 7" x 8"
332. Broadmoor Hotel, The – 1915: 15" x 19"
333. Broadmoor Hotel, The: Large – 1970's
334. Canyon – 1924: 6" X 10"
335. Canyon – 1924: 12" x 15"
336. Cleopatra – 1917: 6 1/2" x 7 1/2"
337. Cleopatra – 1917: 15" x 16"
338. Cleopatra – 1917: 24 1/2" x 28"
339. Daybreak – 1922: 6" x 10"
340. Daybreak – 1922: 10" x 18"
341. Daybreak - 1922: 18" x 30"
342. Dreaming – 1928: 6" x 10"
343. Dreaming – 1928: 10" x 18"
344. Dreaming – 1928: 18" x 30"
345. Dream Garden – 1915: 14" x 24 1/2"
346. Evening – 1922: 6" x 10"
347. Evening – 1922: 12" x 15"
348. Garden Of Allah – 1918: 4 1/2" x 8 1/2"
349. Garden Of Allah – 1918: 9" x 18"
350. Garden Of Allah - 1918: 15" x 30"
351. Garden Of Opportunity – 1925: two side panels
     20 1/2" x 6" – Center panel 20" x 11"
352. Hilltop – 1927: 6" x 10"
353. Hilltop – 1927: 12" x 20"
354. Hilltop – 1927: 18" x 30" or larger
355. Idiot, The – 1910: 8" x 10"
356. Idiot, The – 1910: 12" x 24"
357. Idiot, The – 1910: 8 1/2" x 12"
358. Idiot, The – 1910: 11" x 16"
359. Lute Players – 1924: 6" x 10"
360. Lute Players – 1924: 10" x 18"
361. Lute Players – 1924: 12" x 15"
362. Lute Players – 1924: 18" x 30"
363. Morning – 1926: 6" x 10"
364. Morning – 12" x 15"
365. Page, The – 1928: 10" x 12"
366. Pied Piper, The – 1914: 7" x 21"
367. Prince, The – 1928: 10" x 12"
368. Reveries – 1928: 6" x 10"
369. Reveries – 1928: 10 1/2 x 16
370. Reveries – 1928: 14 1/2" x 22"
371. Romance – 1925: 12" x 24"
372. Royal Gorge Colorado – 1925: 16 1/2" x 20"
373. Rubaiyat – 1917: 4" x 14"
374. Rubaiyat – 1917: 8" x 30"
375. Sing A Song Of Sixpence – 1910: 9" x 21"

Prints

376. Spirit Of Transportation – 1923: 16" x 20"
377. Spirit Of Transportation – 1923: 4" x 5"
378. Stars – 1926: 22 1/2" x 14 1/2"
379. Stars – 1926: 10" x 18"
380. Stars – 1926: 18" x 30"
381. Tranquility – 1936: 9" x 11 1/2"
382. Twilight – 1937: 18" x 22 1/2"
383. White Birch – 1931: 9" x 11"
384. Wild Geese – 1924: 12" x 15"

Scribner's & Sons

385. Acussin Seeks Nicolette – 1905: 11 1/2" x 17"
386. Dinkey-Bird – 1905: 5" x 7"
387. Dinkey-Bird – 1905: 11" x 16"
388. Errant Pan – 1910: 9" x 11"
389. Land Of Make Believe – 1912: 9" x 11"
390. Land Of Make Believe – 1912: 16" x 20"
391. Sugar Plum Tree – 1905: 5" x 7"
392. Sugar Plum Tree – 1905: 11" x 16"
393. With Trumpet & Drum – 1905: 5" x 7"
394. With Trumpet & Drum – 1905: 11" x 16"
395. Wyken, Blinken, & Nod – 1905: 5" x 7"
396. Wyken, Blinken, & Nod – 1905: 11" x 16"

Ladies' Home Journal

397. Air Castles – 1904: 12" x 16"

Miscellaneous Art Prints

398. Alladin & The Wonderful Lamp – 1907: 9" x 11"
399. Atlas – 1908: 9" x 11"
400. Autumn – 1905: 10" x 12"
401. The Brazen Boatman – 1907: 9" x 11"
402. Cadmus – 1909: 9" x 11"
403. Cassim – 1906: 9" x 11"
404. Chimera, The – 1909: 9" x 11"
405. Chiron The Centaru – 1910: 9" x 11"
406. Circes Palace – 1908: 9" x 11"
407. City Of Brass, The – 1905: 9" x 11"
408. Easter – 1905: 8" x 10"
409. Forest Princess – 1916: 11" x 14"
410. Fountain Of Pirene, The – 1907
411. Gardener, The – 1906 & 1907: 12" x 19"
412. Gardener, The – 14" x 19 1/2"

Prints

413. Harvest – 1905: 8" x 10"
414. Hiawatha – 1908: 10" x 6"
415. History Of The Fisherman, The – 1906: 9" x 11"
416. Jack Frost – 1936: 12" x 13"
417. Jason And The Talking Oak – 1908: 9" x 11"
418. The King Of The Black Isles – 1907: 9" x 11"
419. The Lantern Bearers – 1910: 9 1/2" x 11 1/2"
419a. Mid Summer Holiday Number – August, 1897
420. Nature Lover, The – 1911: 10" x 13"
421. Old King Cole – 1896: 6 1/2" x 25"
422. Pandora – 1909: 9" x 11"
422a. Poster Show – 1896
423. Prince Codadad – 1906: 9" x 11"
424. Prosperia & Sea Nymphs – 1910: 9" x 11"
425. Queen Gulnare – 1907: 9" x 11"
426. Quest For The Golden Fleece, The – 1910:
      9" x 11"
427. Search For The Singing Tree, The – 1906: 9" x 11"
428. Sinbad Plots Against The Giant – 1907: 9" x 11"\
429. Spring – 1905: 8" x 10"
430. Story Of A King's Son – 1906: 9" x 11"
431. Summer – 1905: 8" x 10"
432. Sweet Nothings - 1912: 11" x 21"
433. Thanksgiving – 1909: 9" x 11"
434. The Tempest, An Odd Angle Of The Isle - 1909:
      7" x 7"
435. The Tempest, The Phoenix Throne – 1909: 7" x 7"
436. The Tempest, The Strong Based Promontory –
      1909: 7" x 7"
437. The Tempest – 1909: 7" x 7"
438. The Valley Of The Diamonds – 1907: 9" x 11"
439. Whispering Gallery, The – 1912: 11" x 21"
440. White Birch – 1930: 9" x 11"

Magazine Ads

**Scribner's
December 1900**

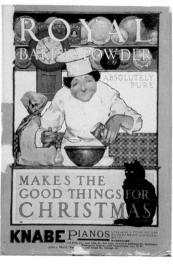

**Scribner's
December 1897**

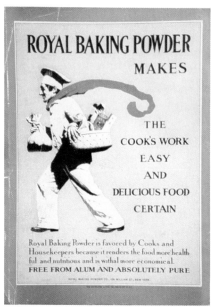

**Scribner's
December 1901**

**Scribner's
August 1901**

46

Magazine Ads

**The Ladies Home Journal
January 1918**

**Collier's
December 22, 1906**

**The Delineator
March 1922**

Ladies Home Journal
December 1918

Magazine Ads

**The Ladies Home Journal
April 1918**

Magazine Ads

Ladies Home Journal
January 1909

Magazine Ads

**The Ladies Home Journal
December 1916**

Magazine Illustrations

**Scribner's
April 1906**

**Collier's
July 21, 1906**

**Ladies Home Journal
October 1930**

**Ladies Home Journal
March 1930**

Magazine Illustrations

Collier's – December 1, 1906

**Collier's
October 13, 1906**

**Collier's
November 3, 1906**

Magazine Illustrations

Century – December 1904

**Scribner's
August 1910**

**Century
December 1901**

Magazine Illustrations

Scribner's – December 1904

Scribner's – December 1904

**Collier's
December 15, 1906**

Magazine Illustrations

Century – November 1904

**Century
May 1902**

**Century
May 1902**

Magazine Illustrations

Scribner's
August 1901

Scribner's
November 1902

Magazine Illustrations

Scribner's
August 1905

Century – November 1904

Magazine Illustrations

Scribner's – August 1901

Scribner's – August 1901

Magazine Illustrations

Scribner's – August 1912

Magazine Illustrations

**Scribner's
December 1903**

Ads & Illustrations

441. American Legion – July 14, 1922
442. American Magazine – September, 1918
443. American Magazine – May, 1921
444. American Magazine – July, 1921
445. American Magazine – May, 1930
446. American magazine – June, 1931
447. American Magazine of Art – January, 1918
448. American Monthly Review – December, 1900
449. American Monthly Review – February, 1918
450. American Printer – October, 1928
451. Architectural League of New York – 1914
452. Architectural League of New York – 1917
453. Art Decorations – October, 1923
454. Art Interchange – June, 1896
456. Art Journal – June, 1903
457. Artist – 1898
458. Atlantic Monthly – June, 1921
459. Atlantic Monthly – July, 1921
460. Atlantic Monthly – December, 1923
461. Atlantic Monthly – December, 1925
462. Atlantic Monthly – April, 1942
463. Book Buyer – April, 1898
464. Bookman – February, 1899
465. Bookman – September, 1900
467. Bookseller – May 1, 1914
468. Bookseller, Newsdealer, & Stationer –
     November 15, 1917
469. Bradley His Book – November, 1896
470. Brush & Pencil – January, 1898
471. Century – December, 1898
472. Century – December, 1899
473. Century – July, 1900
474. Century – December, 1900
475. Century – January, 1901
476. Century – December, 1901
477. Century – May, 1902
478. Century – June, 1902
479. Century – July, 1902
480. Century – August, 1902
481. Century – November, 1902
482. Century – November, 1903
483. Century – December, 1903
484. Century – February, 1904
485. Century – April, 1904
486. Century – August, 1904
487. Century – October, 1904
488. Century – November, 1904

Ads & Illustrations

489. Century – December, 1904
490. Century – March, 1905
491. Century – October, 1905
492. Century – August, 1910
493. Century – November, 1910
494. Century – February, 1911
495. Century – April, 1911
496. Century – April, 1912
497. Century – July, 1912
498. Century – August, 1912
499. Century – December, 1915
500. Century – February, 1918
501. Century – December, 1918
502. Century – June, 1921
503. Century – July, 1921
504. Century – September, 1921
505. Century – February, 1922
506. Century – December, 1923
507. Chicago Tribune – February 2, 1936
508. Christian Herald – March, 1919
509. Collier's – April 30, 1904
510. Collier's – October 29, 1904
511. Collier's – January 21, 1905
512. Collier's – February 25, 1905
513. Collier's – April 8, 1905
514. Collier's – August 12, 1905
515. Collier's – October, 14, 1905
516. Collier's – March 24, 1906
517. Collier's – April 7, 1906
518. Collier's – April 21, 1906
518a. Collier's – July 21, 1906
519. Collier's – September 1, 1906
520. Collier's – October 13, 1906
521. Collier's – October 27, 1906
522. Collier's – November 3, 1906
523. Collier's – December 1, 1906
524. Collier's – December 15, 1906
525. Collier's – December 22, 1906
526. Collier's – January 19, 1907
527. Collier's – February 9, 1907
528. Collier's – March 16, 1907
529. Collier's – March 30, 1907
530. Collier's – May 18, 1907
531. Collier's – June 22, 1907
532. Collier's – September 7, 1907
533. Collier's – November 9, 1907
534. Collier's – January 11, 1908
535. Collier's – January 25, 1908

Ads & Illustrations

536. Collier's – May 16, 1908
537. Collier's – October 31, 1908
538. Collier's – December 12, 1908
539. Collier's – March 27, 1909
540. Collier's – April 24, 1909
541. Collier's – May 1, 1909
542. Collier's – May 15, 1909
543. Collier's – October 16, 1909
544. Collier's – October 23, 1909
545. Collier's – March 5, 1910
546. Collier's – April 23, 1910
547. Collier's – July 23, 1910
548. Collier's – December 10, 1910
549. Collier's – April 8, 1911
550. Cosmopolitan – January, 1901
551. Cosmopolitan – February, 1924
552. Country Calendar – February 27, 1904
553. Country Life – November, 1903
554. Country Life – March, 1904
555. Country Life – July, 1913
556. Country Life – September, 1917
557. Country Life – May, 1918
558. Country Life – August, 1919
559. Critic, The – April 4, 1896
560. Critic, The – May 16, 1896
561. Delineator – March, 1922
562. Everybody's – November, 1901
563. Everybody's – December, 1901
564. Everybody's – May, 1903
565. Farm Journal, The – September, 1925
566. Farmer's Wife, The – November, 1922
569. Good Furniture – February, 1916
570. Good Housekeeping – February, 1924
571. Good Housekeeping – July, 1925
572. Harper's Bazaar – March, 1922
573. Harper's Monthly – December, 1898
574. Harper's Monthly – July, 1921
575. Harper's Monthly – February, 1922
576. Harper's Monthly – December, 1923
577. Harper's Weekly – December 14, 1895
578. Harper's Weekly – April 11, 1896
579. Harper's Weekly – December 8, 1900
580. Harper's Weekly – April 14, 1906
581. Hearst's – March, 1922
582. House & Garden – April, 1904
583. Illustrated London News – August 24, 1907
584. Illustrated London News – November 21, 1910

Ads & Illustrations

585. Illustrated London News – December, 1910
586. Illustrated London News – December, 1913
587. Illustrated London News – December, 1922
588. Independent - November 21, 1907
589. Industrial & Applied Art Books – 1926
590. International Studio – September, 1898
591. International Studio – December, 1899
592. International Studio – July, 1906
593. International Studio – February, 1908
594. International Studio – February, 1909
595. International Studio – January, 1911
596. International Studio – August, 1912
597. Ladies' Home Journal – December, 1902
598. Ladies' Home Journal – February, 1903
599. Ladies' Home Journal – March, 1903
600. Ladies' Home Journal - May, 1903
601. Ladies' Home Journal – July, 1903
602. Ladies' Home Journal – February, 1905
603. Ladies' Home Journal – March, 1905
603a. Ladies' Home Journal – January, 1909
604. Ladies' Home Journal – December, 1911
605. Ladies' Home Journal – May, 1912
606. Ladies' Home Journal – November, 1913
607. Ladies' Home Journal – December, 1915
608. Ladies' Home Journal – March, 1916
609. Ladies' Home Journal – December, 1916
610. Ladies' Home Journal – January, 1918
611. Ladies' Home Journal – April, 1918
612. Ladies' Home Journal – December, 1918
613. Ladies' Home Journal – January, 1919
614. Ladies' Home Journal – December, 1920
615. Ladies' Home Journal – November, 1921
616. Ladies' Home Journal – July, 1925
617. Ladies' Home Journal – March, 1930
618. Ladies' Home Journal - October, 1930
619. Ladies' Home Journal – January, 1931
620. Life – September 13, 1917
621. Life – November 6, 1917
622. Life – May 16, 1918
623. Life – July 6, 1922
624. Life – Janaury 31, 1924
625. Life – October 21, 1938
626. Life – June 24, 1940
627. Life – January 1, 1945
628. Literary Digest – May 11, 1918
629. Magazine of Light – Summer, 1931
630. McCalls – March, 1922
631. McClure's – November, 1904

Ads & Illustrations

Ads & Illustrations

Calendars

**Edison Mazda Lamps
1929**

**Brown & Bigelow
Charles Millar & Sons
Morning Light
1957**

**Charles Millar & Sons
Misty Morn – 1956**

Calendars

**Edison Mazda
Lamps
1926**

**Edison Mazda Lamps
1932**

**Edison Mazda
1923**

Calendars

Brown & Bigelow Co.
Evening Shadow – 1940

Andis Clipper Co.
1958

Brown & Bigelow Co.
Millpond – 1948

Calendars

Brown & Bigelow
Christmas Eve – 1948

Edison Mazda
Lamps
1919

Edison Mazda
Lamps
1921

Calendars

**Edison Mazda Lamps
1931**

**Edison Mazda
Lamps
1928**

Portal Press – 1993

Calendars

**Edison Mazda
Lamps
1920**

**Edison Mazda Lamps
1930**

**BB Calendar
Millpond – 1948**

Calendars

**Edison Mazda
Lamps
1922**

**Edison Mazda Lamps
1934**

**Brown & Bigelow Co.
John Courtney
Peaceful Valley – 1936**

Calendars

Brown & Bigelow
Lindsay Wire Weaving Co.
Early Autumn – 1939

Calendars

Brown & Bigelow

716. Peaceful Valley – 1936: small
716a. Peaceful Valley – 1936: large
717. Peaceful Valley – 1936: x-large
718. Twilight – 1937: small
719. Twilight – 1937: medium
720. Twilight – 1937: large
721. Twilight – 1937: x-large
722. The Glen – 1938: small
723. The Glen – 1938: medium
724. The Glen – 1938: large
725. The Glen – 1938: x-large
726. Early Autumn – 1939: small
727. Early Autumn – 1939: medium
728. Early Autumn – 1939: large
729. Early Autumn – 1939: x-large
730. Evening Shadows – 1940: small
731. Evening Shadows – 1940: medium
732. Evening Shadows - 1940: large
733. The Village Brook – 1941: small
734. The Village Brook – 1941: medium
735. The Village Brook – 1941: large
736. The Village Brook – 1941: x-large
737. Winter Twilight – 1941
737a. Winter Twilight – 1973
738. Thy Templed Hills – 1942: small
739. Thy Templed Hills – 1942: medium
740. Thy Templed Hills – 1942: large
741. Thy Templed Hills – 1942: x-large
742. Silent Night – 1942
742a. Silent Night – 1966
743. A Perfect Day – 1943: small
744. A Perfect Day – 1943: medium
745. A Perfect Day – 1943: large
746. A Perfect Day – 1943: x-large
747. At Close Of Day – 1943
748. Thy Rocks and Rills – 1944: small
749. Thy Rocks and Rills – 1944: medium
750. Thy Rocks and Rills – 1944: large
751. Thy Rocks and Rills – 1944: x-large
752. Eventide – 1944
753. Sunup – 1945: small
754. Sunup – 1945: medium
755. Sunup – 1945: large
756. Sunup – 1945: x-large
758. Valley Of Enchantment - 1946: small
759. Valley Of Enchantment – 1946: medium
760. Valley Of Enchantment – 1946: large
761. Valley Of Enchantment - 1946: x-large

Calendars

Brown & Bigelow

762. The Path To Home – 1946
763. Evening – 1947: small
764. Evening – 1947: medium
765. Evening – 1947: large
766. Evening – 1947: x-large
767. Peace At Twilight – 1947
768. The Millpond – 1948: small
769. The Millpond - 1948: medium
770. The Millpond - 1948: large
771. The Millpond – 1948: x-large
772. Christmas Eve – 1948
773. Christmas Eve – 1971
774. The Village Church – 1949: small
775. The Village Church – 1949: medium
776. The Village Church – 1949: large
777. The Village Church – 1949: x-large
778. Christmas Morning – 1949
778a. Christmas Morning – 1954-60
779. Sunlit Valley – 1950: small
780. Sunlit Valley – 1950: medium
781. Sunlit Valley – 1950: large
782. Sunlit Valley – 1950: x-large
783. A New Day – 1950
784. Daybreak – 1951: small
785. Daybreak – 1951: medium
786. Daybreak – 1951: large
787. Daybreak – 1951: x-large
788. The Twilight Hour – 1951
789. An Ancient Tree – 1952: small
790. An Ancient Tree – 1952: medium
791. An Ancient Tree – 1952: large
792. An Ancient Tree – 1952: x-large
793. Lights Of Welcome – 1952
794. Evening Shadows – 1953: small
795. Evening Shadows – 1953: medium
796. Evening Shadows – 1953: large
797. Evening Shadows – 1953: x-large
798. Peaceful Night – 1953
799. The Old Glen Mill – 1954: small
800. The Old Glen Mill – 1954: medium
801. The Old Glen Mill – 1954: large
802. The Old Glen Mill – 1954: x-large
803. When Day Is Dawning – 1954
804. Peaceful Valley - 1955: small
805. Peaceful Valley – 1955: medium
806. Peaceful Valley – 1955: large
807. Peaceful Valley – 1955: x-large

Calendars

Brown & Bigelow

808. Sunrise – 1955
809. Misty Morn – 1956: small
810. Misty Morn – 1956: medium
811. Misty Morn – 1956: large
812. Misty Morn – 1956: x-large
813. Evening – 1956
814. Morning Light – 1957: small
815. Morning Light – 1957: medium
816. Morning Light – 1957: large
817. Morning Light – 1957: x-large
818. At Close Of Day – 1957
819. New Moon – 1958: small
820. New Moon – 1958: medium
821. New Moon – 1958: large
822. New Moon – 1958: x-large
823. Sunlight – 1958
824. Under Summer Skies - 1959: small
825. Under Summer Skies – 1959: medium
826. Under Summer Skies – 1959: large
827. Under Summer Skies – 1959: x-large
828. Peace At Evening – 1959
829. Sheltering Oaks – 1960: small
830. Sheltering Oaks – 1960: medium
831. Sheltering Oaks – 1960: large
832. Sheltering Oaks – 1960: x-large
834. Twilight – 1961: small
835. Twilight – 1961: medium
836. Twilight – 1961: large
837. Twilight – 1961: x-large
838. Daybreak – 1961
839. Quiet Solitude – 1962: small
840. Quiet Solitude – 1962: medium
841. Quiet Solitude – 1962: large
842. Quiet Solitude – 1962: x-large
843. Evening Shadows – 1962
844. Peaceful Country – 1963: small
845. Peaceful Country – 1963: medium
846. Peaceful Country – 1963: large
847. Peaceful Country – 1963: x-large

P.F. Collier & Son

848. Maxfield Parrish Calendar for 1907 – Spring
849. Maxfield Parrish Calendar for 1907 – Summer
850. Maxfield Parrish Calendar for 1907 – Harvest
851. Maxfield Parrish Calendar for 1907 – Father Time

Calendars

Dodge Publishing Company
852. Business Man's Calendar – 1917
853. Calendar Of Cheer – 1921
854. Calendar Of Friendship – 1925
855. Contentment Calendar – 1925
856. Sunlit Road Calendar – 1925
857. Business Man's Calendar – 1925
858. Business Man's Calendar – 1926
859. Calendar Of Cheer – 1926
860. Contentment Calendar – 1926
861. Calendar Of Sunshine – 1926
862. Sunlit Road Calendar – 1926
863. Calendar Of Friendship – 1926

General Electric Mazda Lamps
864. Dawn – 1918
865. Spirit Of The Night – 1919
866. Prometheus – 1920
867. Primitive Man – 1921
868. Egypt – 1922
869. Lamp Seller Of Bagdad – 1923
870. Venetian Lamplight – 1924
871. Dream Light – 1925
872. Enchantment – 1926
873. Reverie – 1927
874. Contentment – 1928
875. Golden Hours – 1929
876. Ecstasy – 1930
877. Waterfalls – 1931
878. Solitude – 1932
879. Sunrise – 1933
880. Moonlight – 1934

Thomas D. Murphy Company
881. Sunrise – 1937
882. Only God Can Make A Tree – 1938
883. Rock Of Ages – 1939
884. White Birch – 1941
885. Hilltop or (Thy Woods & Tempted Hills) – 1942: small
886. Hilltop or (Thy Woods & Tempted Hills) – 1942: large
886a. Charles Millar & Sons – 1956
886b. Charles Millar & Sons – 1957
886c. Andis Clipper Co. – 1958
886d. Portal Press – 1993
886e. John Courtney – 1936

Miscellaneous

Menu – St. Regis Hotel, N.Y.C. 1991

Postcard – The Broadmoor
1940's

Miscellaneous

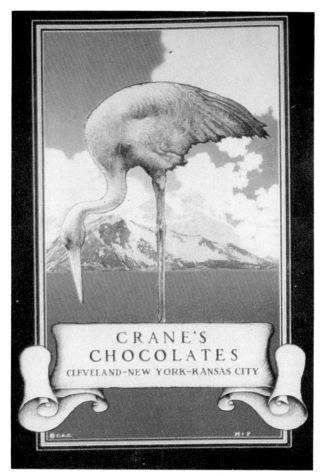

Candy Box – Teens

Crane Candy Box – Teens

Miscellaneous

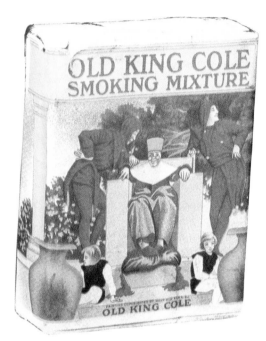

Tobacco Package – 1926

**Match Box – St. Regis Hotel N.Y.C.
1991**

Miscellaneous

**Stamp – Brill Brothers
1915**

Playing Cards – 1924

**Soldier Ten Pins Game – Parker Brothers
1923**

Miscellaneous

887. Bookmatches – The Broadmoor 1960's
888. Cookie Tin – The Broadmoor 1970's – 1980's
889. Djer-Kiss Waltz – Sheet Music 1925
890. Metal Signs – Mazda Edison, Knave of Hearts
892. Signatures on typed letters, checks, etc.
893. Stamp - Brill Bros. 1915-60
894. Tape Measure – 1920's
895. Wallpaper Border – Fisk Tire
896. Set of 4 Collier's Art Prints – 1910 from The Arabian
　　　Knights, orig. mats. King of Black Isles, Cassim
　　　in the Cave, Circe's Palace, Prince Codadad
897. Pocket Calendar - Prometheus 2" x 3"
897a. Postcard – The Broadmoor - 1940

Crane Chocolates – Candy Boxes
898. A Crane – Teens
899. Garden of Allah, The – Teens
900. Rubaiyat, The – Teens

Old King Cole
901. Cigar Box Labels - 1920's
902. Match Boxes – St. Regis, N.Y.C. – 1991
903. Menu - St. Regis – 1991
904. Stationary – 1920's
905. Tie Rack – 1920's
906. Tobacco Pack – 1926

Playing Cards – Priced Mint
907. And Night Is Fled
908. Contentment
909. Dawn
910. Ectasy I
911. Egypt
912. Enchantment
913. In The Mountains
914. Lamp Seller of Bagdad
915. New Moon
916. Reveries
917. Spirit of Night, The
918. Sweltering Oaks
919. Venetian Lamplighter, The
920. Waterfall, The

Miscellaneous

Puzzles

921. Broadmoor, The 1940's
922. Daybreak – 1970's
923. Garden of Allah – Teens
924. Knave & Lady Violetta – 1920's
925. Prince, The – 1920's
926. Queens Page, The – 1920's

Signs

927. Metal Sign – Knaves: Edison Mazda

Toys

928. Bowling Pins – 1930's
929. Comic Toy Soldiers – 1920's
930. Kiddie Komical Kut-outs – 1920's
931. M.P. Soldier with air gun – 1913
932. Soldier Ten Pins, (10-9" pins) – 1920's

Book Plates

"Cicogna"

"Boboli"

"Villa Campi"

"The Theater at
Villa Gori"

Book Plates

"Villa Chigi"

"Vicobello"

"Camberaia"

"Villa Gori"

Book Plates

"Villa Merici"

"Isola Bella"

Book Plates

"Three Shepherds"
The Golden Treasury of
Songs and Lyrics
1911

"Pierrot"
The Golden Treasury of
Songs and Lyrics
1911

"With Trumpet & Drum"
Poems of Childhood
1904

"Snuffle-Shoon &
Amber-Locks"
Poems of Childhood
1904

Book Plates

"See in Things"
Poems of Childhood
1904

"The Little Peach"
Poems of Childhood
1904

"The Fly-Away Horse"
Poems of Childhood
1904

Book Plates

"Manager Draws The Curtain"
Knave of Hearts

"Romance"
Knave of Hearts – 1924

Book Plates

"The Broadmoor" – 1927

Book Plates

**"The Young King of
the Black Isles"
Arabian Nights – 1909**

**"Prince Agib"
Arabian Nights**

**"Fisherman and the Genie"
Arabian Nights – 1909**

**"Ali Baba"
Arabian Nights – 1909**

Book Plates

"Talking Bird"
Arabian Nights – 1909

"The History of Copadad and
His Brothers
Arabian Nights – 1909

"Sin Bad"
Arabian Nights – 1909

Book Plates

"Gulnare of the Sea"
Arabian Nights – 1909

"The City of Brass"
Arabian Nights – 1909

"Second Voyage of Sinbad"
Arabian Nights – 1909

"Prince Agib"
Arabian Nights – 1909

Book Plates

"I took the old fellow to the station." . . ."
The Golden Age

"A great book open on his knee, . . . a score or so disposed within easy reach" . . ."
The Golden Age

". . .'It was easy . . . to transport yourself in a trice to the heart of a tropical forest."
The Golden Age

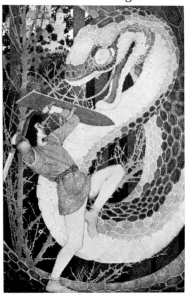

"Once more were damsels rescued, dragons disembowelled, and giants' . . . etc."
The Golden Age

Book Plates

"I'm Jason . . . and this is
the Argo, . . . and we're
just going through the
Hellespont" . . . "
The Golden Age

" . . . On to the garden wall,
which led in its turn to the
roof of an out-house."
The Golden Age

"I drew it out and carried it
to the window, to examine
it in the failing light."
The Golden Age

"Out into the brimming sun-
bathed world I sped . . ."
The Golden Age

Book Plates

The Arabian Night, Their Best-Known Tales – 1909

The Fisherman
The Arabian Nights
The Talking Bird
The Fisherman and the Genie
The Young King of the Black Isles
Gulnare of the Sea
Aladdin
Prince Agib, Landing of the Brazen Boatman
Prince Agib, The Story of the King's Son
The City of Brass
The Story of Ali Baba and the Forty Thieves
The History of Codadad and His Brothers
Second Voyage of Sinbad
Third Voyage of Sinbad

The Golden Age – 1899

The Golden Age
The Burglers
The Olympians
A Holiday
A Whitewashed Uncle
Alarums and Excursions
Finding of A Princess
Sawdust and Sin
Young Adam Cupid
A Harvesting
Snowbound
What They Talked About
The Argonauts
The Roman Road
The Secret Drawer
Exit Tyrannus
The Blue Room
A Falling Out
Lusisti Satis

The Golden Treasury of Songs and Lyrics - 1911

Spring
Autumn
The Lantern Bearers
Three Shepherds
Summer

Book Plates

Harvest
Pierrot
Spring
Easter

Italian Villas and Their Gardens

Villa Campi, near Florence
The Reservoir, Villa Falconieri, Frascati
The Cascade, Villa Torlonia, Frascati
Boboli Garden, Florence
Villa Gamberaia, near Florence
Villa Corsini, Florence
Vicobello, Siena
La Palazzina (Villa Gori)
The Theatre at La Palazzina, Siena
The Dome of St. Peter's, from the Vatican Gardens
Villa Medici, Rome
Villa Pia - In the Gardens of the Vatican
Villa Chigi, Rome
Villa d'Este, Tivoli
The Pool, Villa d'Este, Tivoli
Villa Lante, Bagnaia
Villa Scassi, Genoa
A Garden-niche, Villa Scassi, Genoa
Villa Cicogna, Bisuschio
Villa Isola Bella, Lake Maggiore
In The Gardens of Isola Bella, Lake Maggiore
Villa Pliniana, Lake Como
Gateway of the Botanic Garden, Padua
View of Val San Zibio, near Battaglia
Val San Zibio, near Battaglia
Villa Valmarana, Vicenza

The Knave of Hearts – 1925

The Knave of Hearts
Romance
This Is The Book Of
Lady Violetta about to Make the Tarts
The Knave of Hearts (The Mask)
The Characters
The Manager Draws the Curtain
Two Chefs at Table
Two Pastry Cooks: Blue Hose and Yellow Hose
Chef Carrying Cauldron

Book Plates

Entrance of Pompdebile, King of Hearts
Chef between Two Lobsters
Lady Ursula Kneeling before Pompdebile, King of Hearts
The Youth and the Frog
The Six Little Ingredients
Violetta and Knave Examining the Tarts
The Gardener Wheeling Vegetables
The King and the Chancellor at Kitchen Door
Two Cooks Peeling Potatoes
The Knave
Fool in Green
The King Tastes the Tarts
The Serenade
The Knave Watches Violetta Depart
The End, The Manager Bows

Mother Goose in Prose – 1897

Little Boy Blue
The Black Sheep
Old King Cole
The Wond'rous Wise Man
Jack Horner
The Man in the Moon
Little Bo-Peep
Tommy Tucker
Tom, the Piper's Son
Humpty Dumpty
The Wise Men of Gotham

Poems of Childhood – 1904

With Trumpet and Drum
The Sugar-Plum Tree
Wynken, Blynken, and Nod
The Little Peach
The Dinkey-Bird
The Fly-Away Horse
Shuffle-Shoon and Amber-Locks
Seein' Things

A Wonder Book and Tanglewood

Circe's Palace
The Argonauts in Quest of the Golden Fleece

Book Plates

Jason and the Talking Oak
Pandora
Atlas
Bellerophon by the Fountain of Pirene
The Fountain of Pirene
Cadmus Sowing the Dragon's Teeth
Circe's Palace
Proserpina
Jason and His Teacher
The Argonauts in Quest of the Golden Fleece

Price Guide

All items priced in this guide are for items in very good condition. Pieces that are stained, torn, with holes or folded (cracked) are worth much less. Items in mint condition such as in tubes or boxes never opened are worth much more.

Dealers will not pay collector prices so you must figure 40-50% off list price if selling to dealer.

Remember, this is only a guide. L-W Books or the author assumes no liability because of loss or gain in using these prices. Items may vary from area to area, so keep in mind this is only a guide.

Magazine Covers		
1 – $50	28 – $75	56 – $75
2 – $75	29 – $75	57 – $75
3 – $75	30 – $75	58 – $40
4 – $75	31 – $60	59 – $60
5 – $75	32 – $75	60 – $60
6 – $75	33 – $60	61 – $80
7 – $75	34 – $100	62 – $75
8 – $75	35 – $75	63 – $75
9 – $75	36 – $75	64 – $75
10 – $75	37 – $60	65 – $60
11 – $75	38 – $75	66 – $60
12 - $75	39 – $75	67 – $60
13 – $75	40 – $75	68 – $60
14 – $50	41 – $90	69 – $60
15 – $75	42 – $80	70 – $60
16 – $55	43 – $75	71 – $75
17 – $75	44 – $75	72 – $75
18 – $60	45 – $75	73 – $75
19 – $60	46 – $75	74 – $75
20 – $75	47 – $75	75 – $40
21 – $75	48 – $75	76 – $75
22 – $60	49 – $75	77 – $75
23 – $60	50 – $75	78 – $75
24 – $75	51 – $75	79 – $75
25 - $60	52 – $110	80 – $75
26 – $75	53 – $75	81 – $70
27 – $60	54 – $60	82 – $60
	55 – $60	83 – $75

84 – $80	127a – $80	172 – $25
85 – $75	128 – $70	173 – $25
86 – $80	129 – $70	174 – $60
87 – $75	130 – $55	175 – $50
88 – $60	131 – $55	176 – $100
89 – $100	132 – $120	177 – $50
90 – $100	133 – $65	178 – $40
91 – $75	134 – $60	179 – $25
92 – $75	135 – $65	180 – $25
93 – $75	136 – $95	181 – $25
94 – $100	137 – $100	182 – $25
95 – $100	138 – $100	183 – $25
96 – $100	139 – $100	184 – $25
97 – $100	140 – $100	185 – $25
98 – $75	142 – $125	186 – $25
99 – $75	143 – $100	187 – $25
100 – $75	144 – $100	188 – $25
101 – $75	145 – $100	189 – $25
102 – $75	146 – $75	190 – $25
103 – $75	147 – $100	191 – $25
104 – $75	148 – $90	192 – $25
105 – $75	149 – $125	193 – $25
106 – $75	150 – $100	193a – $25
107 – $75	151 – $85	194 – $25
108 – $60	152 – $100	195 – $25
109 – $60	153 – $100	196 – $25
110 – $60	154 – $125	197 – $25
111 – $75	155 – $110	198 – $25
112 – $190	156 – $110	199 – $25
113 – $200	157 – $110	200 – $25
114 – $200	158 – $100	201 – $25
115 – $200	159 – $115	202 – $25
116 – $90	160 – $100	203 – $25
117 – $100	161 – $100	204 – $25
118 – $100	162 – $100	205 – $25
119 – $150	163 – $75	206 – $25
120 – $150	164 – $75	207 – $25
121 – $150	165 – $65	208 – $25
122 – $150	166 – $65	209 – $25
123 – $150	167 – $50	209a – $100
124 – $150	168 – $50	210 – $125
125 – $150	169 – $50	211 – $100
126 – $90	170 – $50	212 – $150
127 – $85	171 – $100	213 – $150

214 – $150

215 – $125

216 – $150

217 – $100

218 – $150

219 – $150

220 – $100

221 – $100

222 – $100

223 – $100

224 – $50

225 – $22

226 – $75

227 – $70

Books

228 – $60

229 – $100

230 – $70

231 – $150

232 – $350

233 – $70

234 – $55

235 – $25

236 – $40

237 – $60

238 – $90

239 – $100

240 – $50

241 – $100

242 – $60

243 – $300

244 – $25

245 – $50

246 – $100

247 – $260

248 – $100

249 – $100

250 – $80

251 – $100

252 – $195

253 – $40

254 – $50

255 – $40

256 – $50

257 – $40

258 – $80

259 – $35

260 – $40

261 – $250

262 – $100

263 – $95

264 – $700

265 – $1200

266 – $10

267 – $300

268 – $45

269 – $55

270 – $60

271 – $60

272 – $90

273 – $225

274 – $30

275 – $1400

276 – $195

277 – $40

278 – $125

279 – $100

280 – $350

281 – $150

282 – $70

283 – $150

284 – $125

285 – $9.95

286 – $200

287 – $50

288 – $115

289 – $100

290 – $120

291 – $40

292 – $45

293 – $180

294 – $20

295 – $100

296 – $70

297 – $75

298 – $100

299 – $200

300 – $125

301 – $200

302 – $25

Posters

303 – $1500

304 – $1595

305 – $975

306 – $2000

307 – $2000

308 – $1050

309 – $700

310 – $1000

311 – $1000

312 – $975

313 – $1250

314 – $1100

315 – $650

316 – $670

317 – $750

318 – $665

319 – $525

320 – $850

321 – $1800

322 – $2000

323 – $775

324 – $1500

325 – $850

326 – $425

327 – $525

328 – $1650

329 – $1600

330 – $450

Prints

Reinthal & Newman

331 – $125

332 – $400

333 – $100

334 – $150

335 – $275

336 – $275

337 – $725

338 – $750

339 – $100
340 – $130
341 – $350
342 – $100
343 – $275
344 – $650
345 – $495
346 – $150
347 – $280
348 – $100
349 – $145
350 – $365
351 – $900
352 – $120
353 – $350
354 – $750
355 – $100
356 – $100
357 – $50
358 – $30
359 – $130
360 – $200
361 – $300
362 – $675
363 – $150
364 – $225
365 – $225
366 – $825
367 – $300
368 – $125
369 – $240
370 – $650
371 – $900
372 – $525
373 – $225
374 – $675
375 – $825
376 – $625
377 – $300
378 – $850
379 – $500
380 – $850
381 – $150
382 – $300

383 – $95
384 – $245

Prints
Scribner's & Sons
385 – $575
386 – $85
387 – $200
388 – $250
389 – $125
390 – $500
391 – $70
392 – $175
393 – $65
394 – $150
395 – $90
396 – $325

Prints
Ladies' Home Journal
397 – $275

Prints
Miscellaneous
398 – $120
399 – $145
400 – $190
401 – $95
402 – $150
403 – $110
404 – $125
405 – $125
406 – $130
407 – $125
408 – $125
409 – $175
410 – $200
411 – $250
412 – $300
413 – $100
414 – $225
415 – $125
416 – $100

417 – $100
418 – $120
419 – $210
419a – $
420 – $250
421 – $1000
422 – $125
422a – $
423 – $125
424 – $125
425 – $125
426 – $125
427 – $125
428 – $125
429 – $125
430 – $125
431 – $165
432 – $275
433 – $175
434 – $125
435 – $125
436 – $125
437 – $100
438 – $125
439 – $300
440 – $150

Ads & Illustrations
441 – $25
442 – $80
443 – $40
444 – $35
445 – $35
446 – $35
447 – $40
448 – $25
449 – $50
450 – $35
451 – $35
452 – $35
453 – $30
454 – $35
456 – $25

457 – $40	502 – $35	545 – $35
458 – $40	503 – $35	546 – $35
459 – $40	504 – $35	547 – $50
460 – $40	505 – $35	548 – $50
461 – $35	506 – $35	549 – $35
462 – $35	507 – $30	550 – $35
463 – $50	508 – $80	551 – $50
464 – $40	509 – $25	552 – $35
465 – $40	510 – $25	553 – $35
467 – $35	511 – $25	554 – $35
468 – $50	512 – $25	555 – $35
469 – $100	513 – $25	556 – $60
470 – $50	514 – $25	557 – $60
471 – $35	515 – $25	558 – $85
472 – $35	516 – $25	559 – $85
473 – $35	517 – $35	560 – $35
474 – $35	518 – $35	561 – $100
475 – $35	518a – $40	562 – $35
476 – $35	519 – $35	563 – $35
477 – $35	520 – $35	564 – $35
478 – $35	521 – $35	565 – $50
479 – $35	522 – $35	566 – $50
480 – $35	523 – $40	569 – $35
481 – $65	524 – $65	570 – $35
482 – $50	525 – $35	571 – $35
483 – $35	526 – $35	572 – $75
484 – $35	527 – $60	573 – $35
485 – $35	528 – $35	574 – $35
486 – $35	529 – $40	575 – $35
487 – $35	530 – $35	576 – $35
488 – $35	531 – $70	577 – $200
489 – $40	532 – $35	578 – $200
490 – $20	533 – $60	579 – $150
491 – $50	534 – $40	580 – $35
492 – $35	535 – $50	581 – $80
493 – $35	536 – $50	582 – $35
494 – $50	537 – $50	583 – $35
495 – $60	538 – $35	584 – $100
496 – $35	539 – $35	585 – $125
497 – $35	540 – $50	586 – $100
498 – $35	541 – $50	587 – $100
499 – $45	542 – $50	588 – $35
500 – $35	543 – $70	589 – $35
501 – $35	544 – $35	590 – $35

591 – $35	634 – $35	679 – $100
592 – $35	635 – $60	680 – $100
593 – $35	636 – $35	681 – $100
594 – $35	637 – $35	681a – $50
595 – $35	638 – $35	682 – $50
596 – $35	639 – $100	683 – $50
597 – $35	640 – $100	684 – $30
598 – $35	641 – $35	685 – $40
599 – $40	642 – $50	686 – $50
600 – $35	643 – $25	687 – $50
601 – $35	644 – $25	688 – $50
602 – $35	645 – $25	689 – $50
603 – $35	646 – $25	690 – $50
603a – $35	647 – $100	691 – $50
604 – $35	648 – $100	692 – $50
605 – $35	649 – $125	693 – $50
606 – $35	650 – $75	694 – $50
607 – $35	651 – $50	695 – $35
608 – $35	652 – $50	696 – $35
609 – $35	653 – $50	697 – $35
610 – $100	654 – $50	698 – $35
611 – $35	655 – $50	699 – $35
612 – $100	656 – $50	700 – $35
613 – $100	657 – $50	701 – $35
614 – $75	658 – $50	702 – $35
615 – $100	659 – $50	703 – $75
616 – $50	661 – $100	704 – $75
617 – $50	662 – $100	705 – $75
618 – $50	663 – $75	706 – $75
619 – $50	664 – $75	707 – $75
620 – $60	665 – $35	708 – $75
621 – $60	666 – $50	709 – $75
622 – $60	667 – $50	710 – $35
623 – $35	668 – $35	711 – $35
624 – $100	669 – $50	712 – $35
625 – $35	670 – $35	713 – $75
626 – $35	671 – $35	714 – $95
627 – $35	672 – $75	715 – $95
628 – $35	673 – $100	
629 – $125	674 – $100	**Calendars**
630 – $100	675 – $100	**Brown & Bigelow**
631 – $100	676 – $100	716 – $50
632 – $35	677 – $100	716a – $175
633 – $35	678 – $100	717 – $220

718 – $70	761 – $285	804 – $40
719 – $150	762 – $225	805 – $125
720 – $190	763 – $50	806 – $175
721 – $290	764 – $70	807 – $250
722 – $50	765 – $165	808 – $100
723 – $160	766 – $280	809 – $60
724 – $175	767 – $200	810 – $150
725 – $390	768 – $60	811 – $250
726 – $60	769 – $110	812 – $300
727 – $150	770 – $170	813 – $100
728 – $225	771 – $350	814 – $50
729 – $275	772 – $200	815 – $125
730 – $75	773 – $60	816 – $150
731 – $150	774 – $45	817 – $250
732 – $250	775 – $120	818 – $150
733 – $50	776 – $190	819 – $40
734 – $140	777 – $250	820 – $100
735 – $275	778 – $200	821 – $150
736 – $380	778a – $60	822 – $200
737 – $200	779 – $70	823 – $100
737a – $60	780 – $115	824 – $60
738 – $60	781 – $160	825 – $100
739 – $200	782 – $175	826 – $150
740 – $150	783 – $195	827 – $225
741 – $295	784 – $40	828 – $150
742 – $225	785 – $125	829 – $50
742a – $60	786 – $150	830 – $100
743 – $40	787 – $285	831 – $100
744 – $125	788 – $125	832 – $150
745 – $160	789 – $40	834 – $30
746 – $300	790 – $150	835 – $60
747 – $150	791 – $200	836 – $100
748 – $50	792 – $300	837 – $175
749 – $75	793 – $175	838 – $135
750 – $175	794 – $45	839 – $30
751 – $325	795 – $135	840 – $50
752 – $160	796 – $180	841 – $100
753 – $45	797 – $250	842 – $150
754 – $135	798 – $225	843 – $125
755 – $175	799 – $75	844 – $30
756 – $315	800 – $150	845 – $75
758 – $50	801 – $250	846 – $100
759 – $110	802 – $300	847 – $200
760 – $200	803 – $150	

Calendars
P.F. Collier & Son
848 – $300
849 – $300
850 – $300
851 – $300

Calendars
Dodge Publishing Company
852 thru 863 with box and ribbon are all
$75

Calendars
General Electric Mazda Lamps
864 thru 880
Priced with full pad.
Small $350-500
Large $700-1000
(Without calendar much less.)

Calendars
Thomas D. Murphy Company
881 thru 886e
Average price is $75 to $100

Miscellaneous
887 – $10
888 – $35
889 – $50
890 – $1000
892 – $150+
893 – $60
894 – $200
895 – $Rare
896 – $150
897 – $20

897a – $20

Crane Chocolates Candy Boxes
898 – $200
899 – $250
900 – $250

Old King Cole
901 – $67.50
902 – $5
903 – $30
904 – $100
905 – $100
906 – $100

Playing Cards
PRICED MINT
907 thru 920
$150 to $200
a pack mint.

Puzzles
921 – $75
922 – $20
923 – $200
924 – $200
925 – $250
926 – $250

Signs
927 – $1000

Toys
928 – $1000
929 – $2000
930 – $1500
931 – $3000
932 – $2500

Book Plates
The Arabian Nights, Their Best-Known Tales – 1909
Average Price
$50 each

The Golden Treasury of Songs and Lyrics – 1911
Average Price
$50 each

Italian Villas and Their Gardens
Average Price
$30 each

The Knave of Hearts – 1925
Average Price
$100 each

Mother Goose in Prose – 1897
Average Price
$60 each

Poems of Childhood – 1904
Average Price
$40 each

A Wonder Book and Tanglewood
Average Price
$40 each

Buy – Sell

GWENS ANTIQUES
P.O. Box 936
Adamstown, PA 19501
Phone # (215) 484-0487

Meeting customers through the mail since 1972
Jon Alk
2606 River Lane • Green Bay, Wisconsin 54301

112

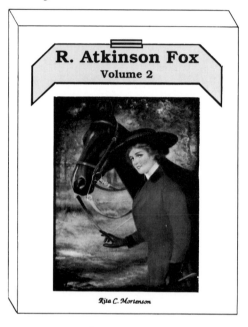